I0483527

AUTOMATIC DRAWINGS
AND SURREAL PAINTINGS

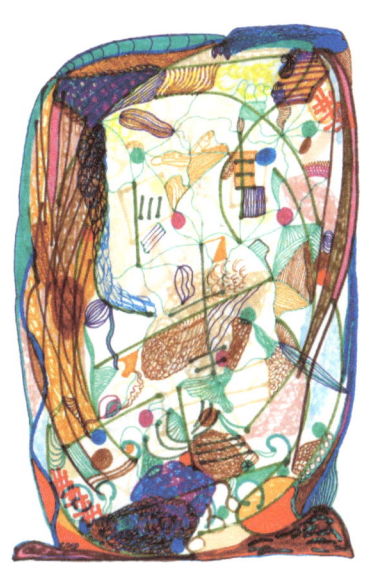

Camilia MacPherson, Ph.D., D.Th.
2016

INTRODUCTION

These small and miniature drawings and paintings have multiple images. To understand the meaning conveyed, it is important to view the drawings and paintings from all angles as well as varying depths.

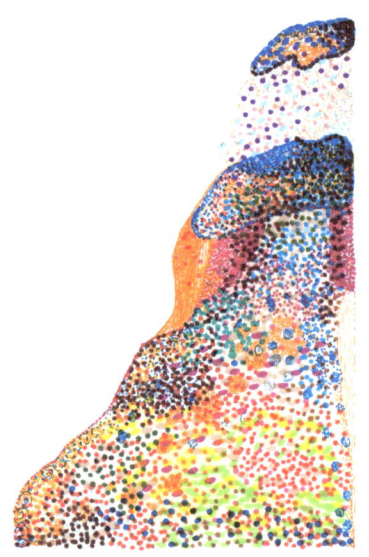

All Rights Reserved
© 2016 by Dr. Camilia MacPherson
ISBN-13: 978-1530377626
Email: tamaracpublishers@icloud.com

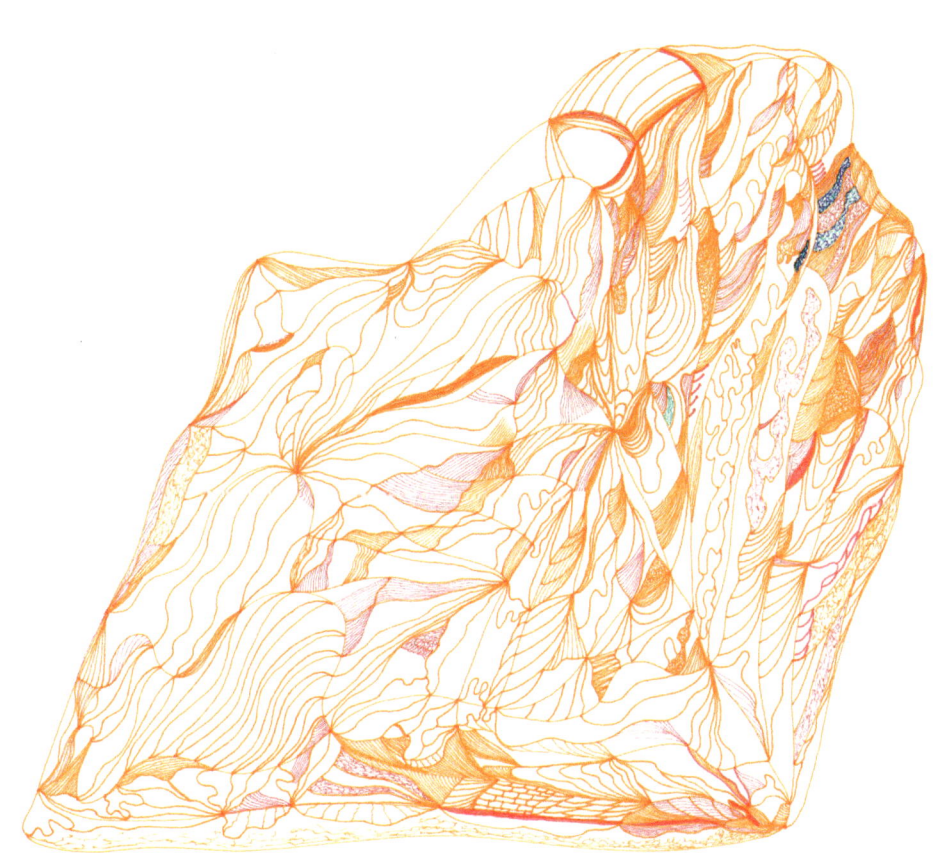

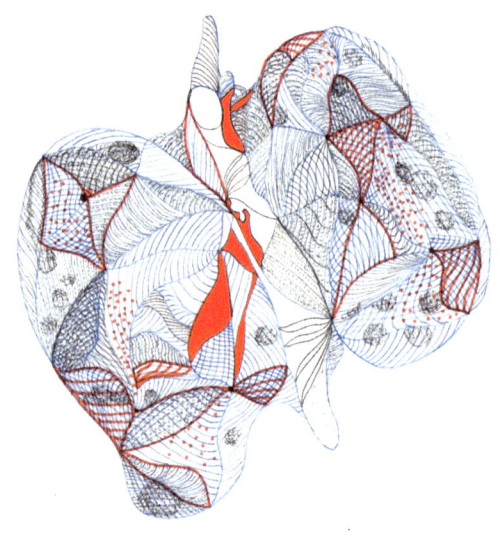

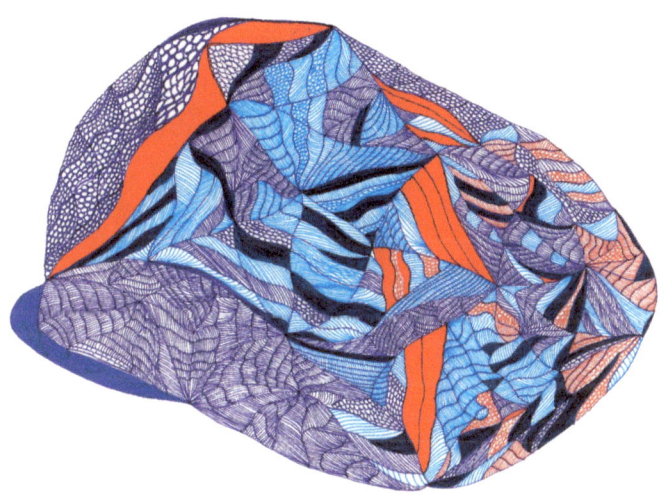

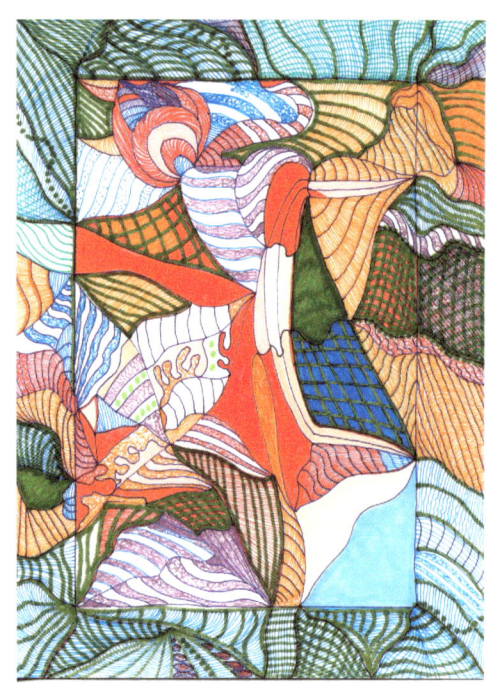

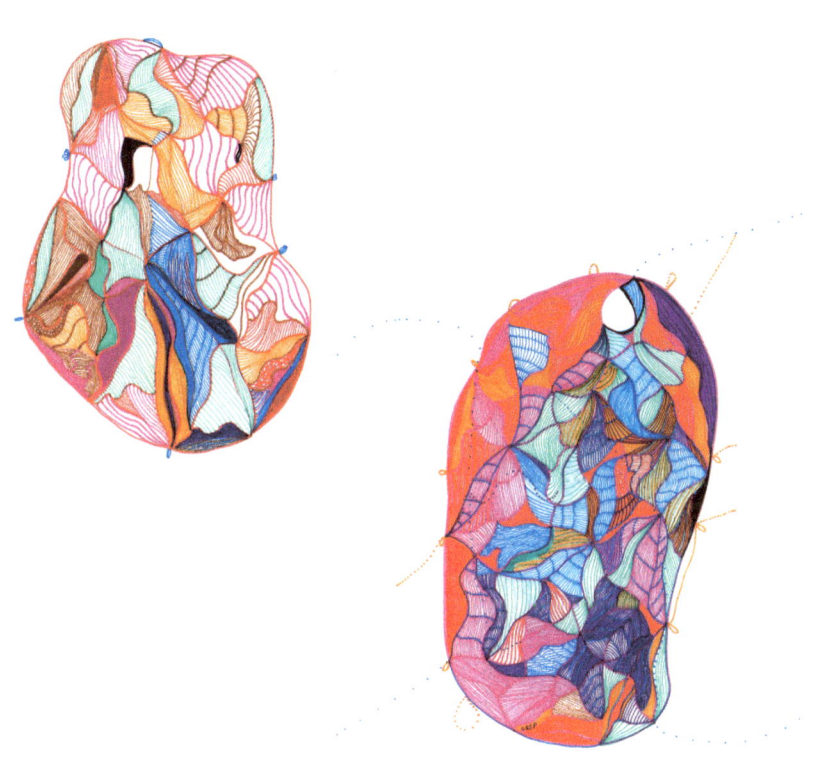

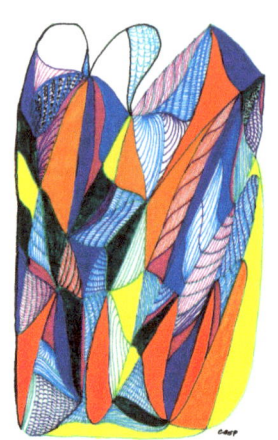
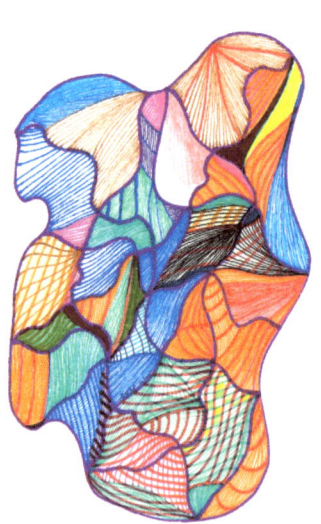

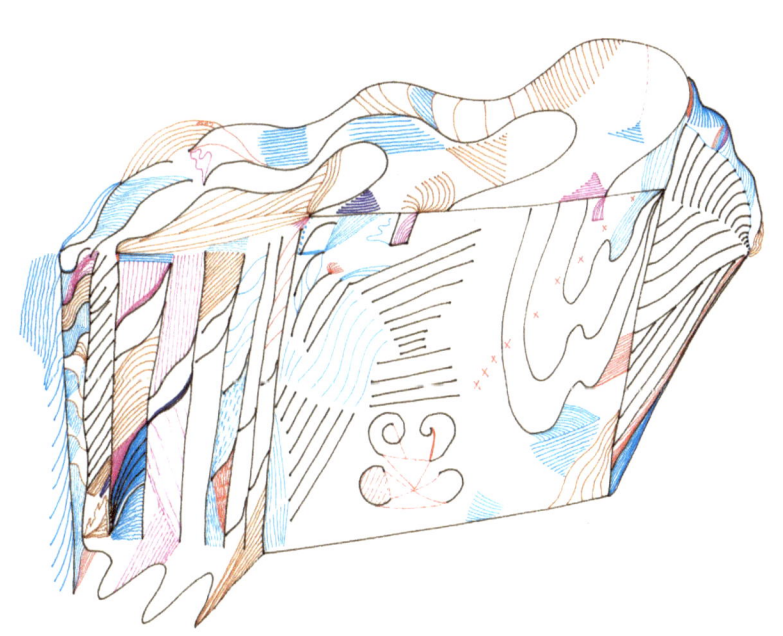

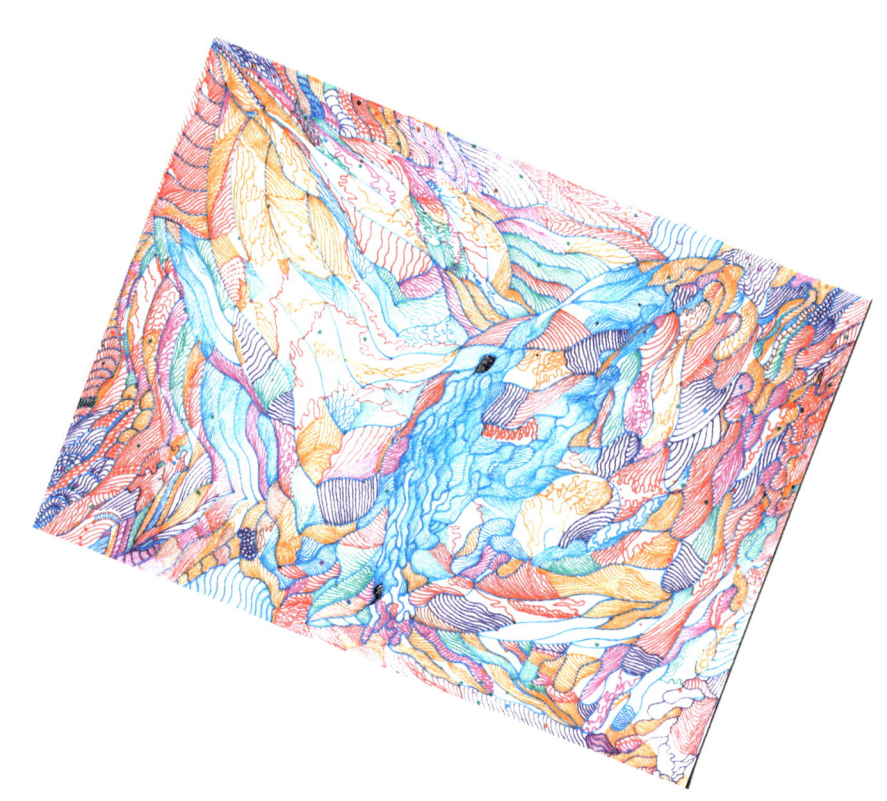

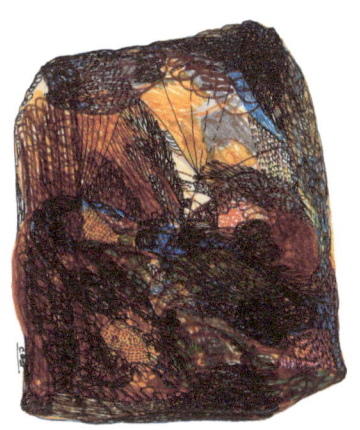

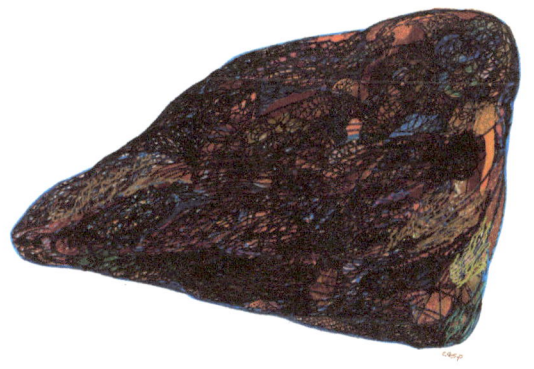

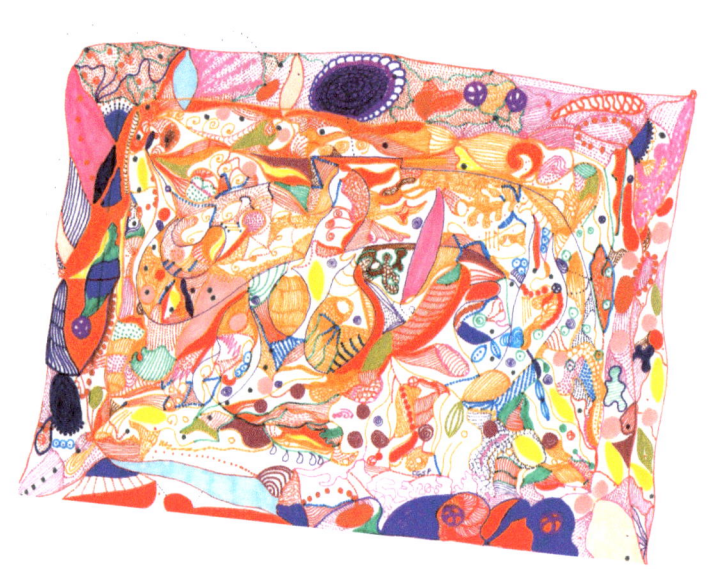

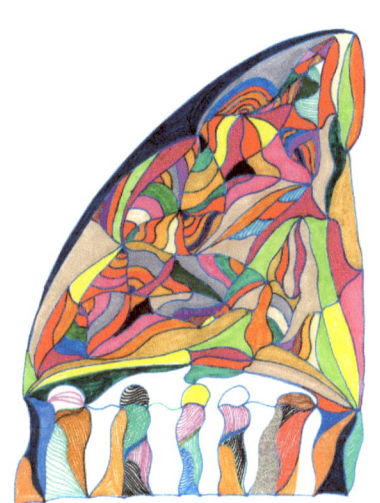

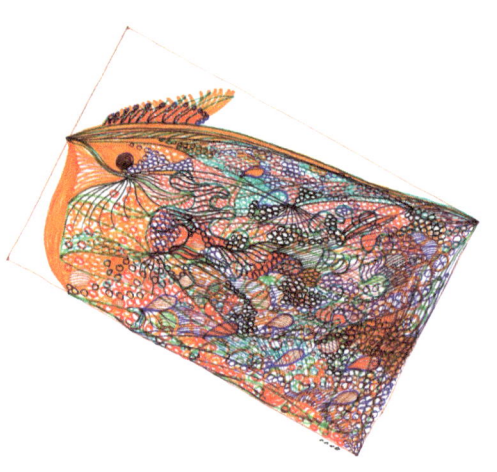

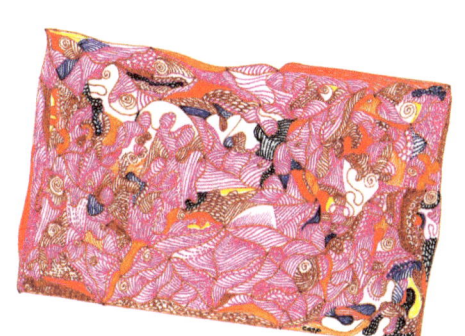

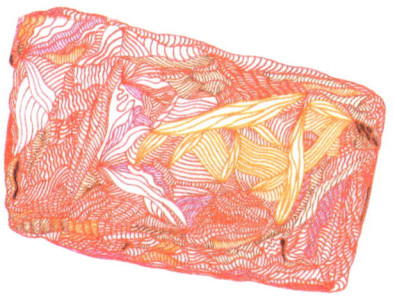

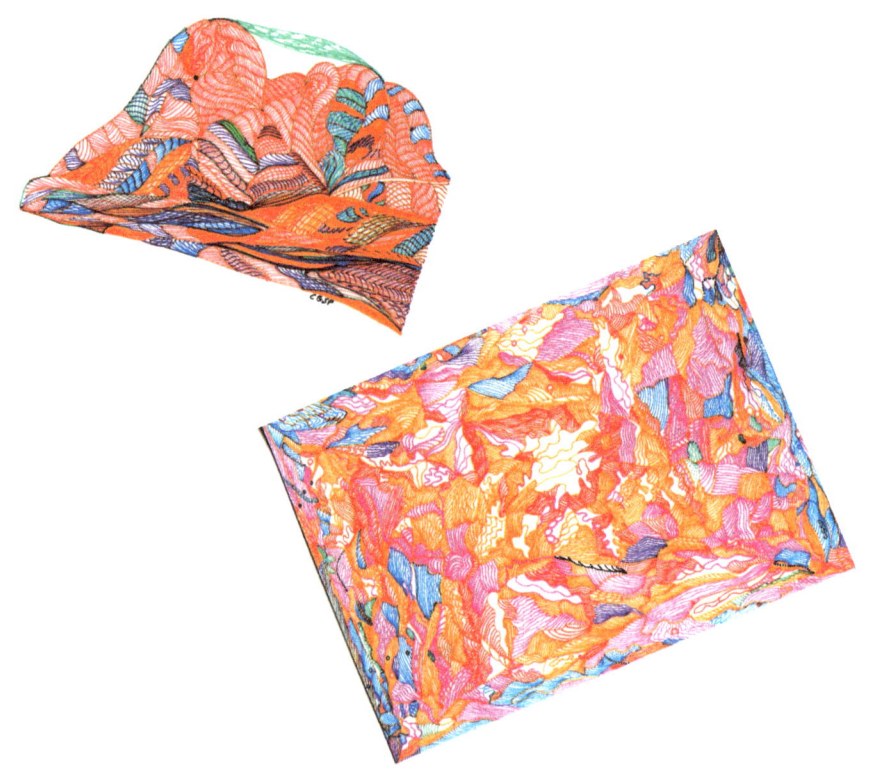

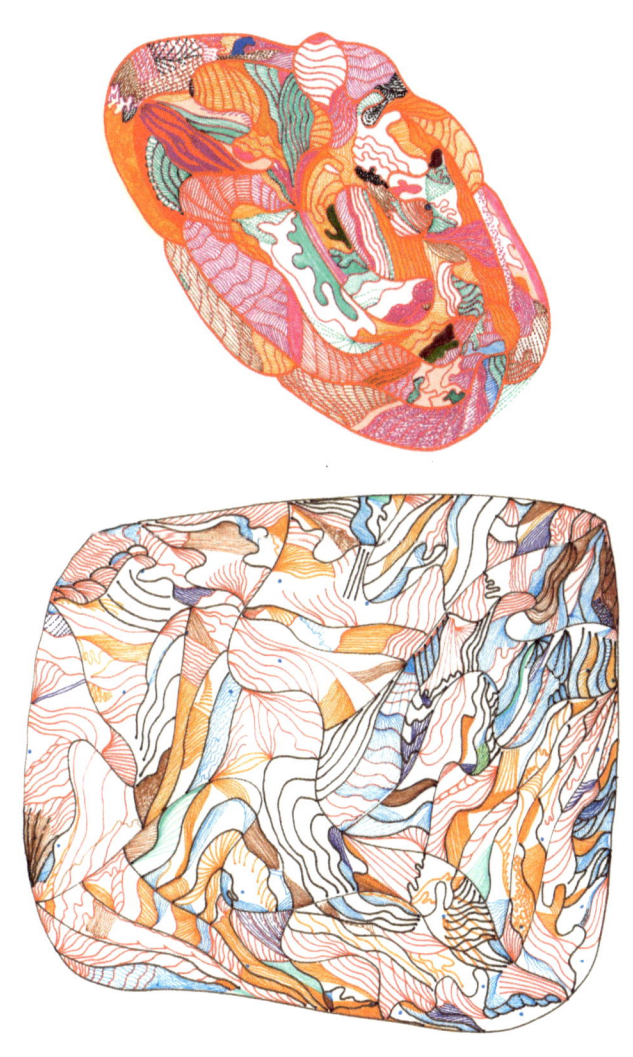

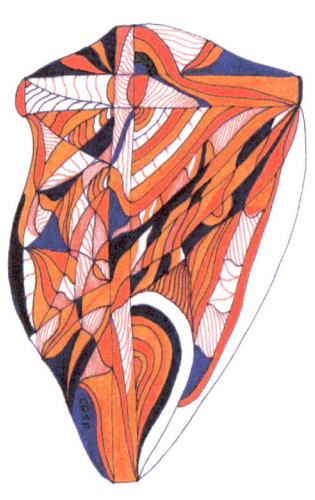

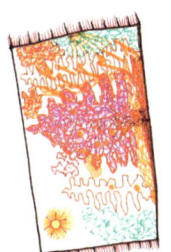
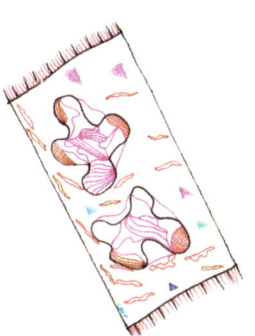

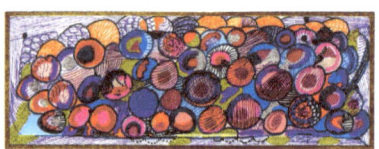

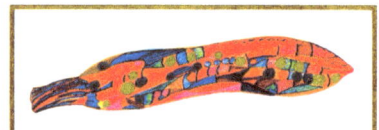

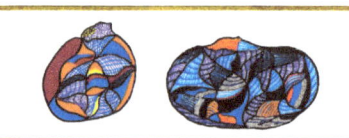

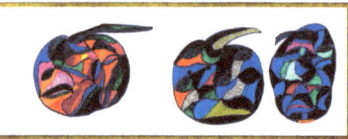

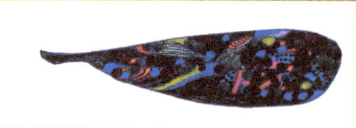

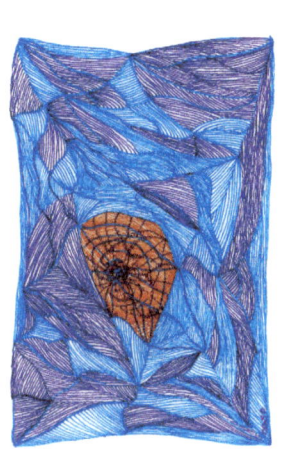

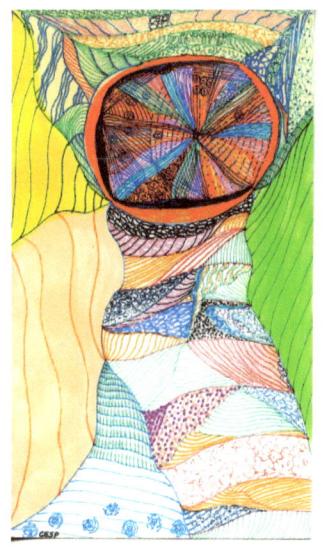

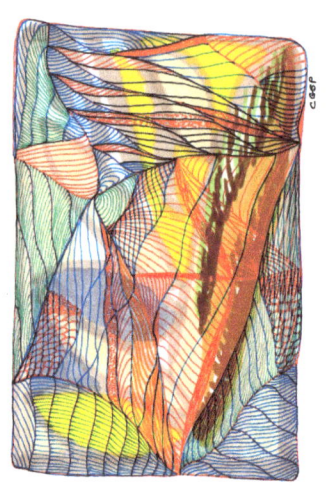

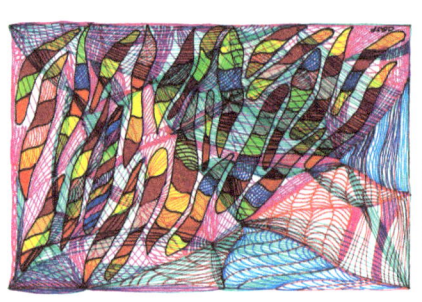

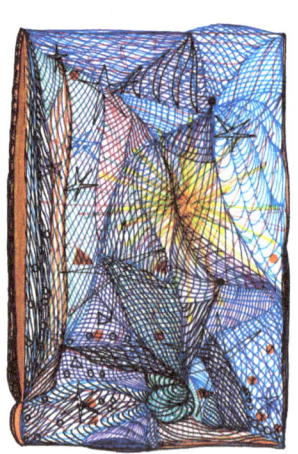

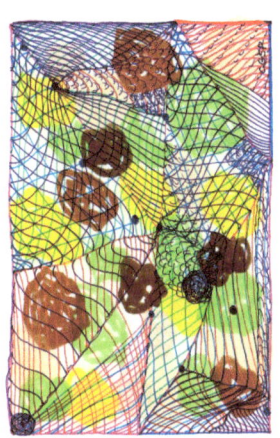
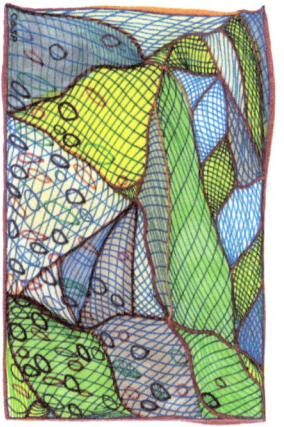

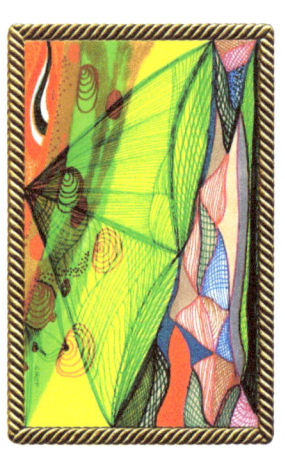
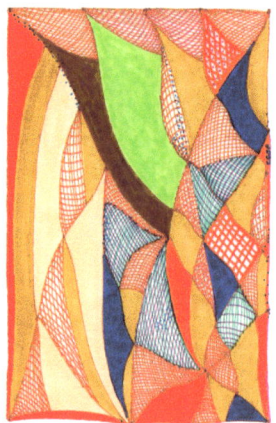

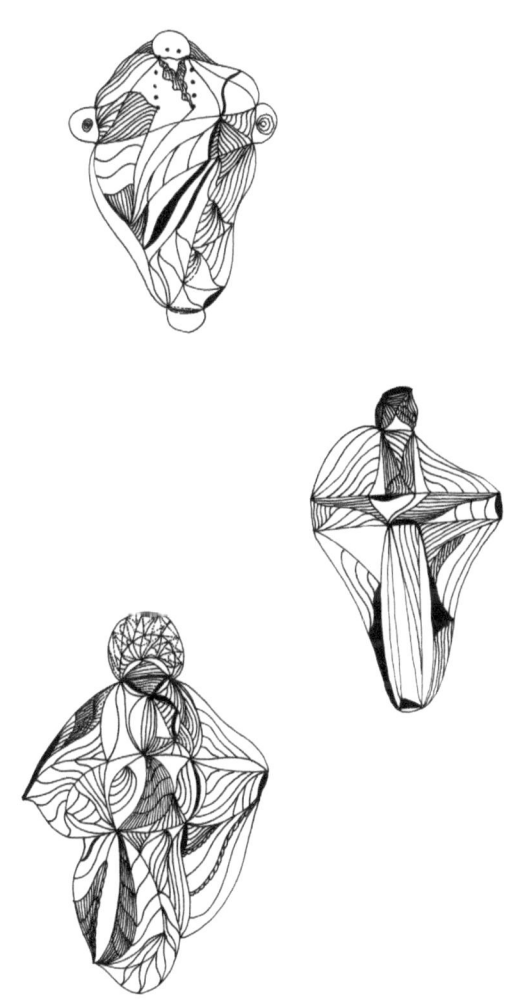

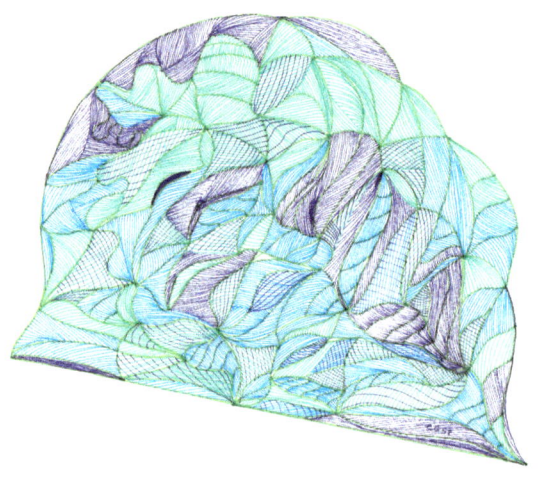

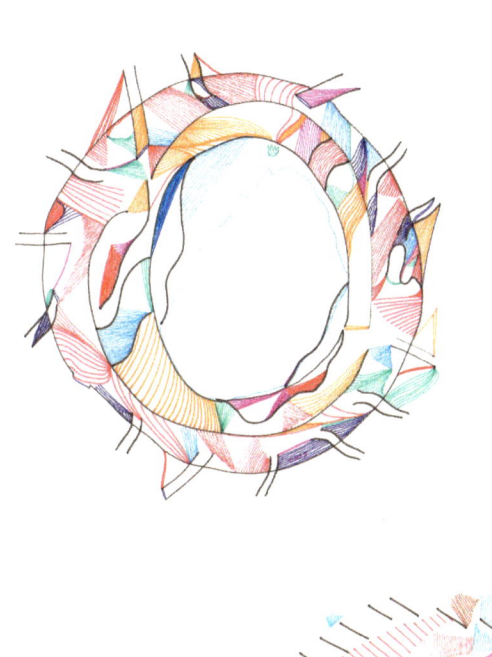

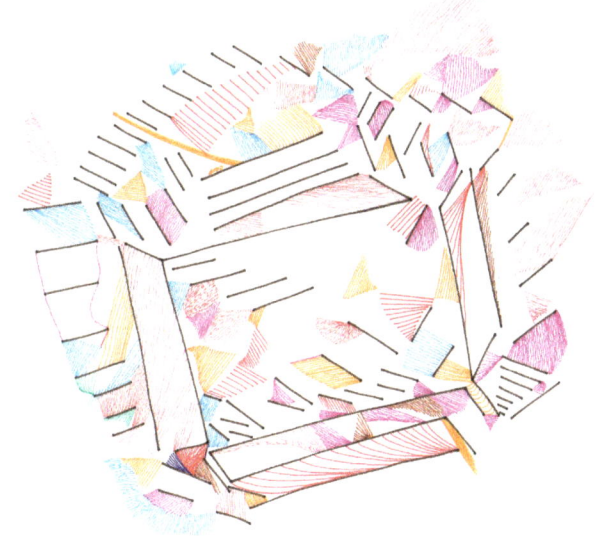

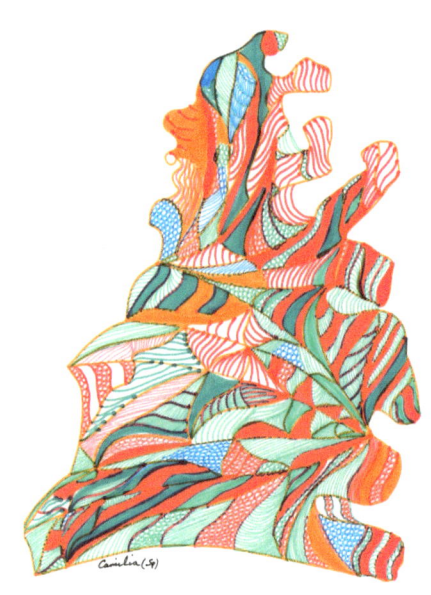

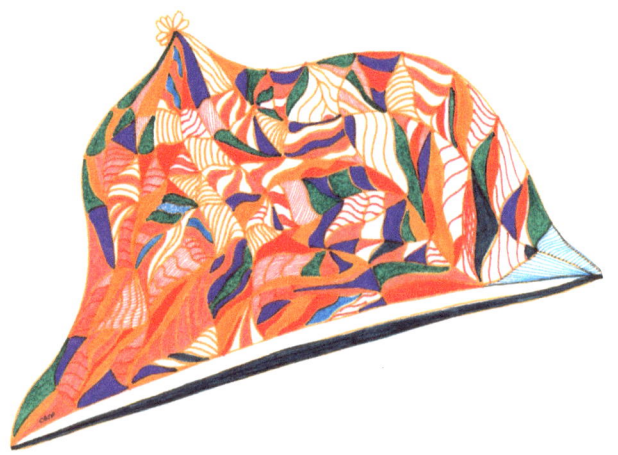

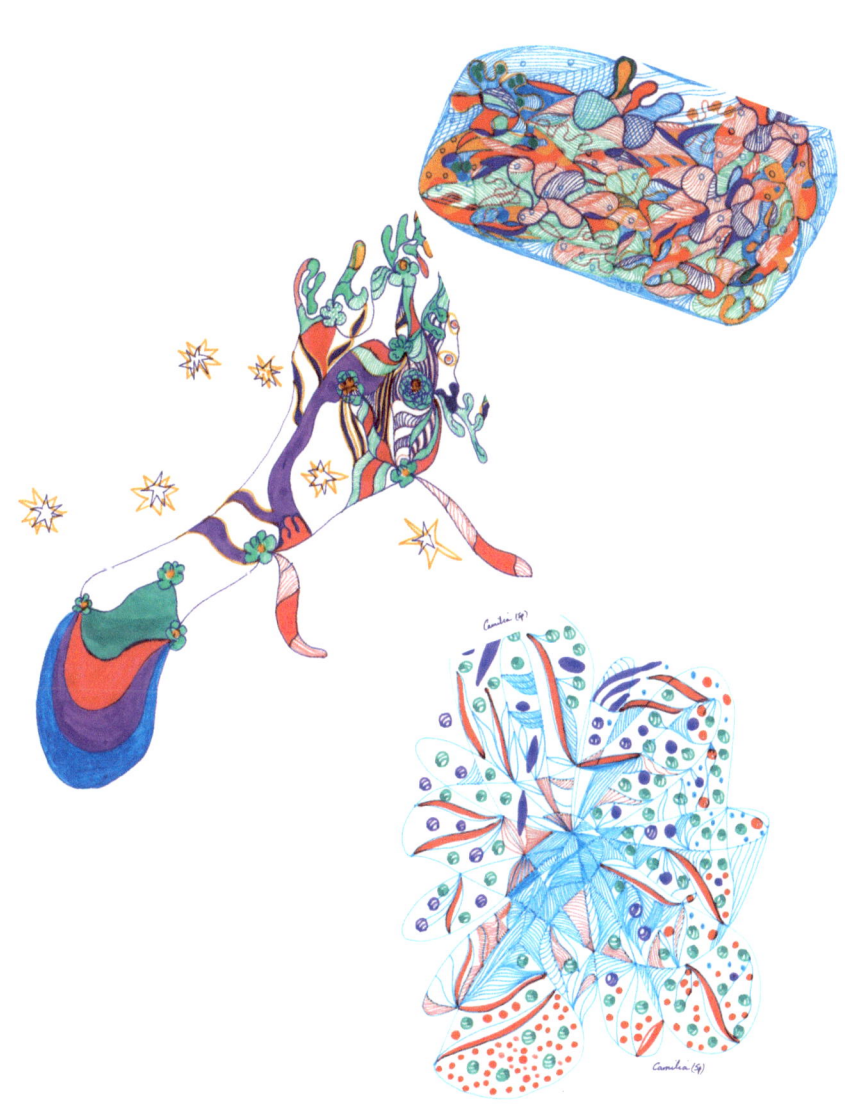

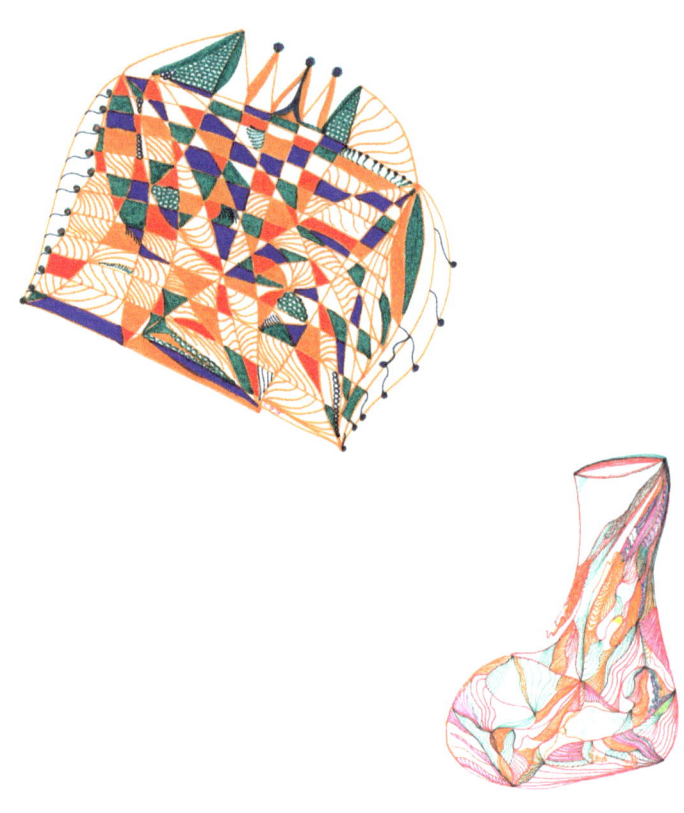

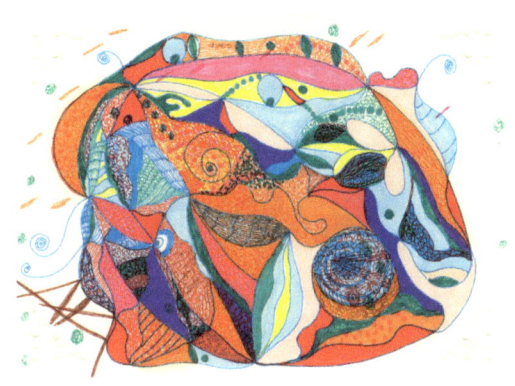

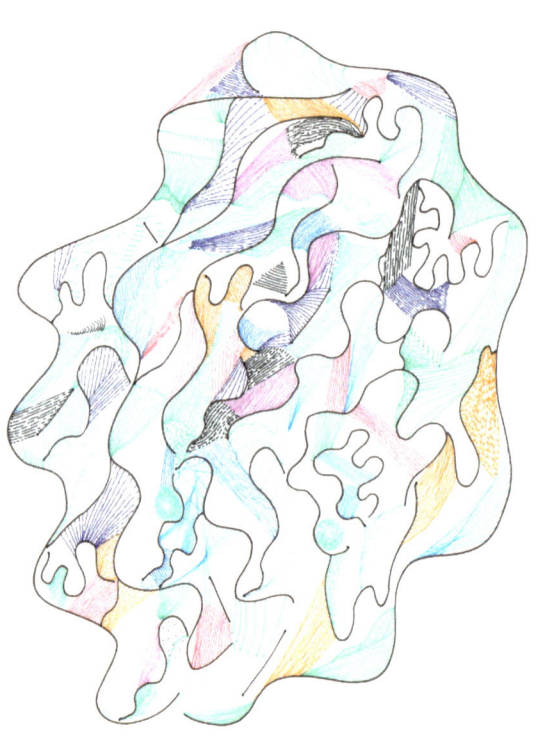

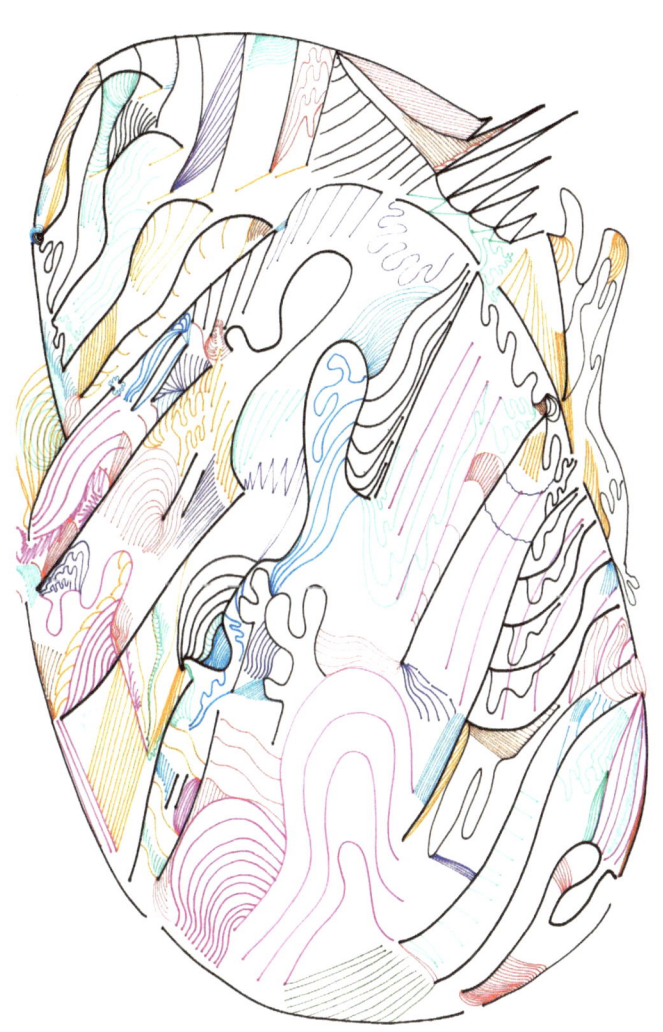

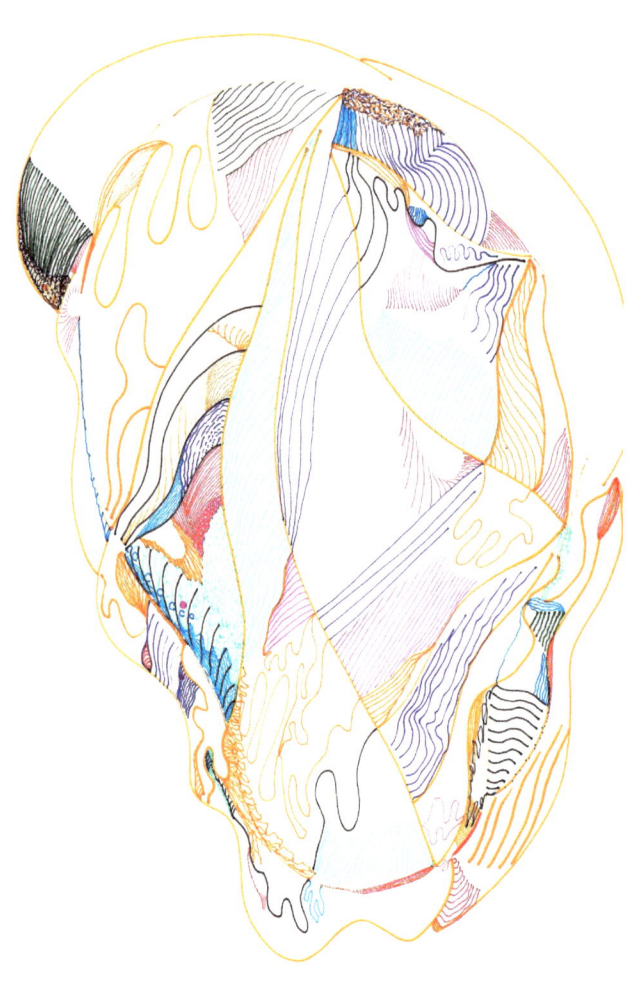

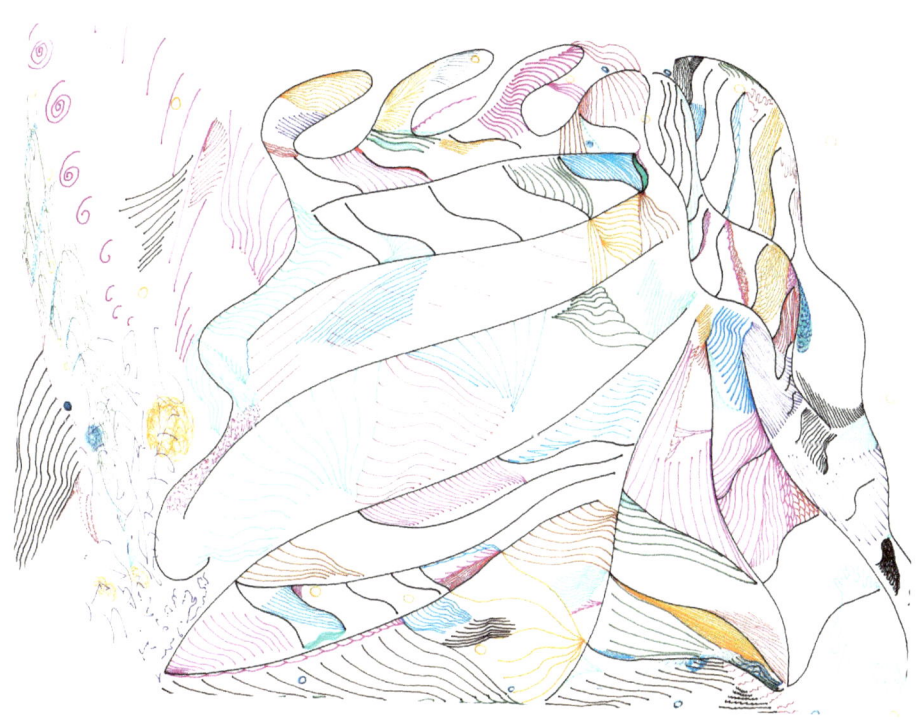

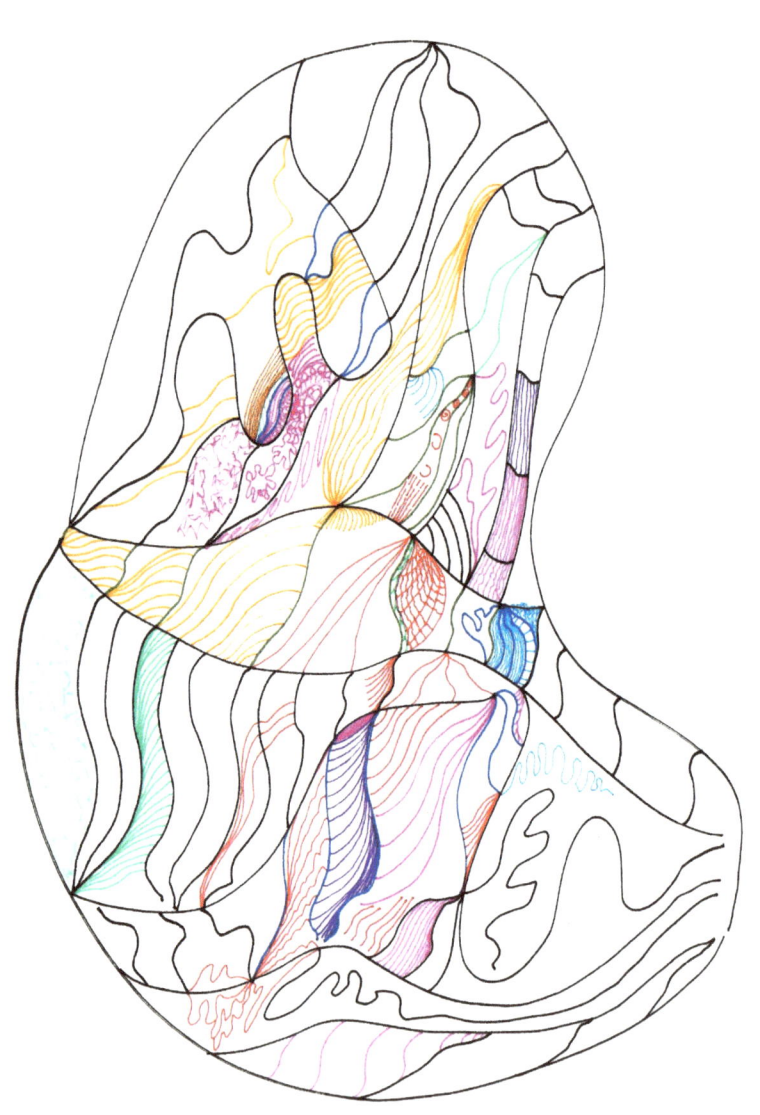

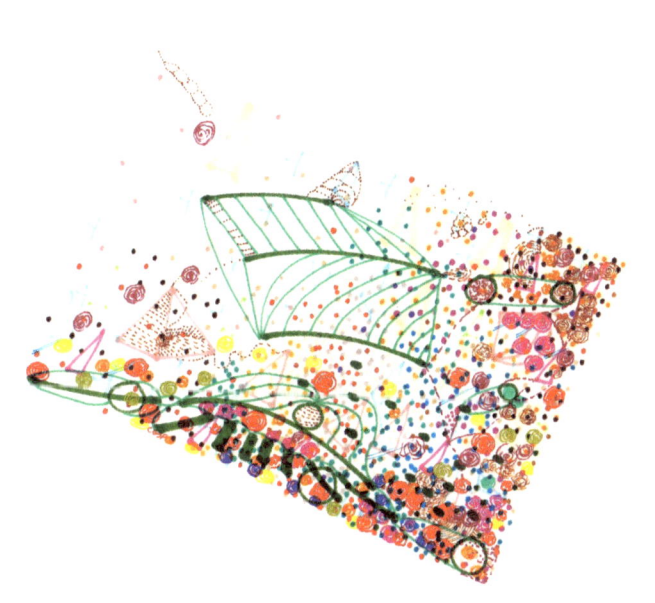

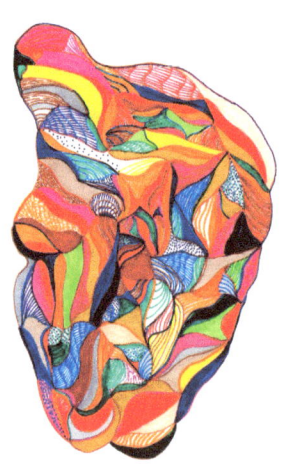

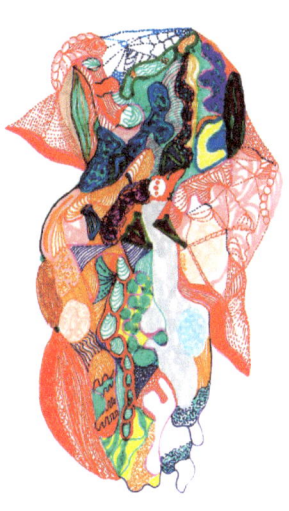

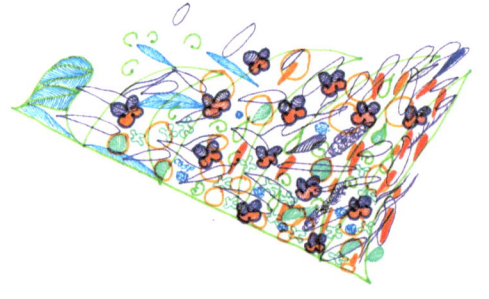

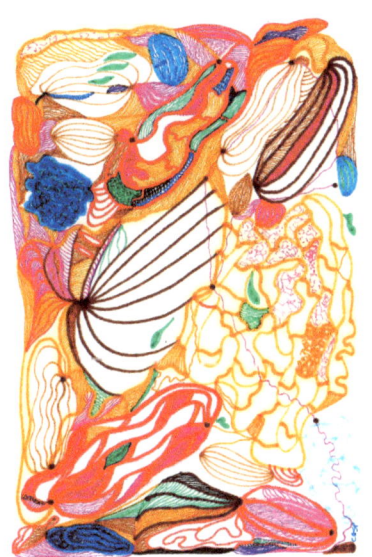

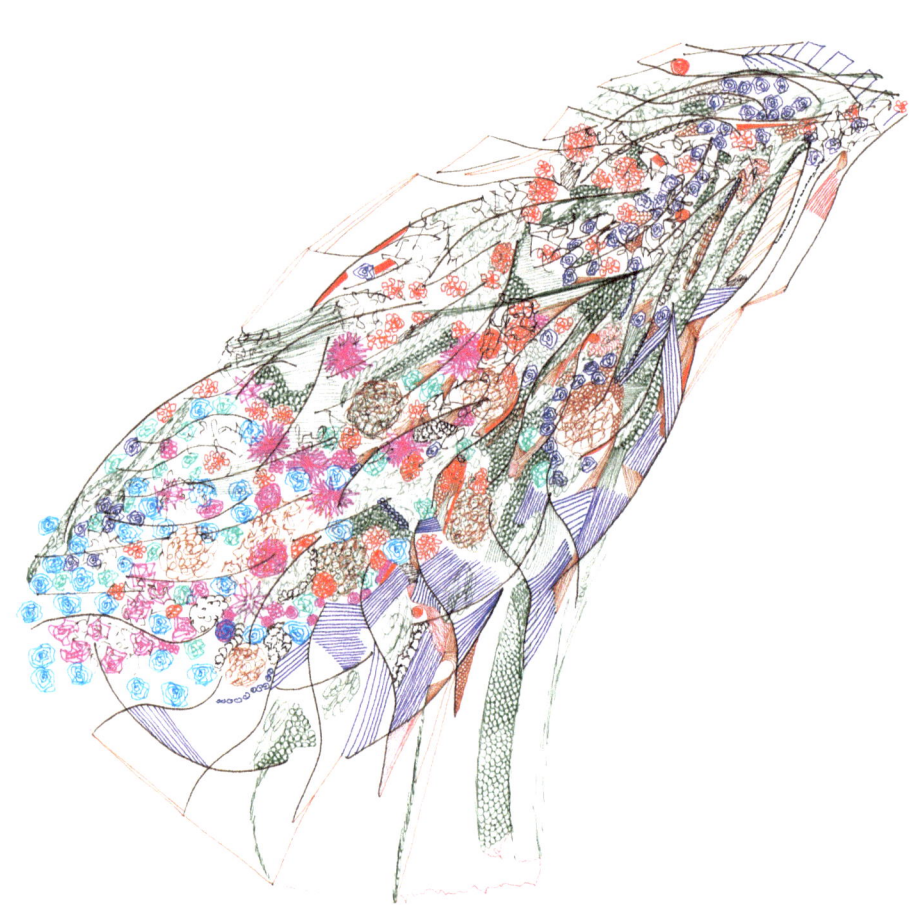

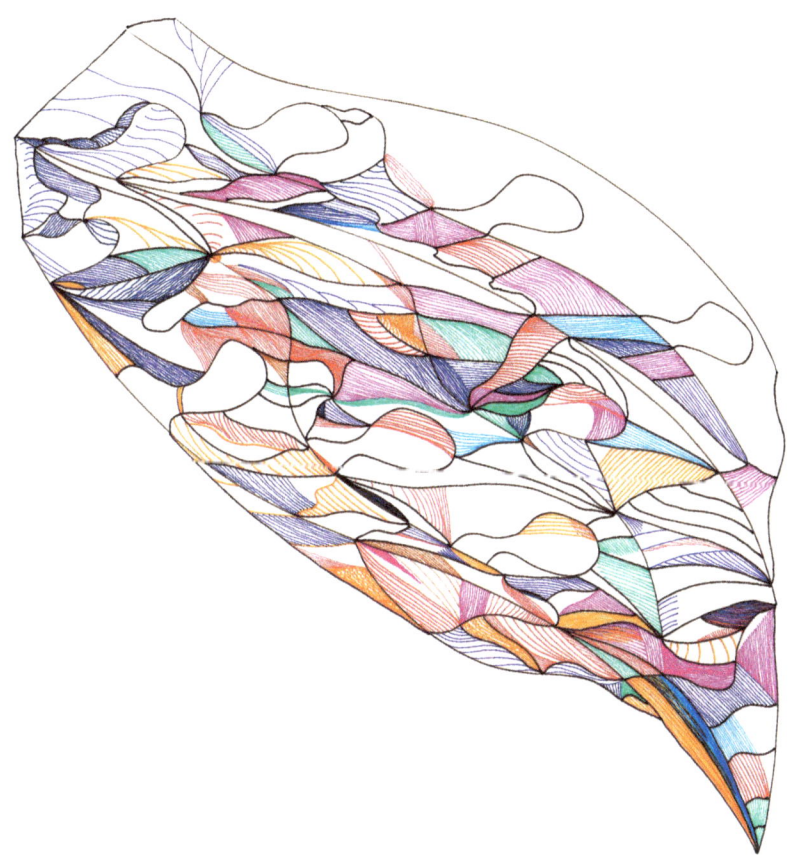

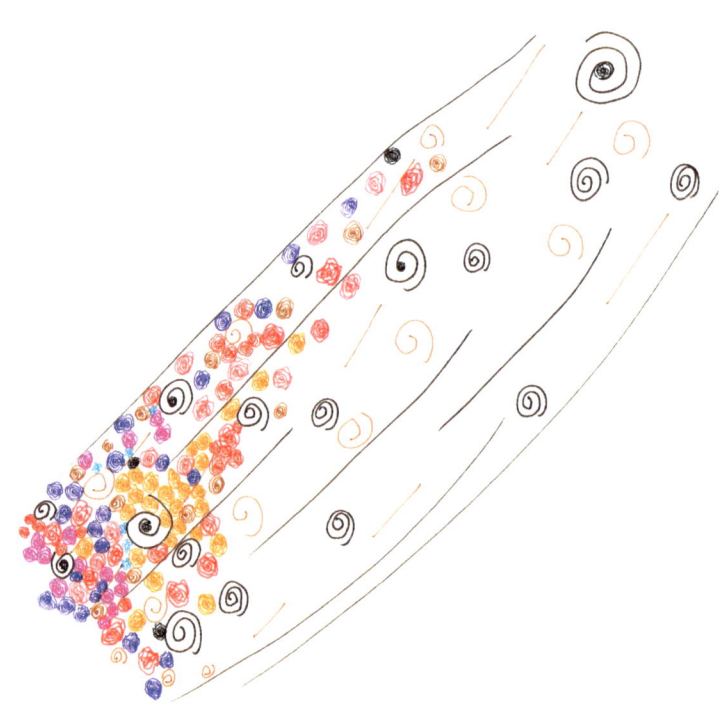

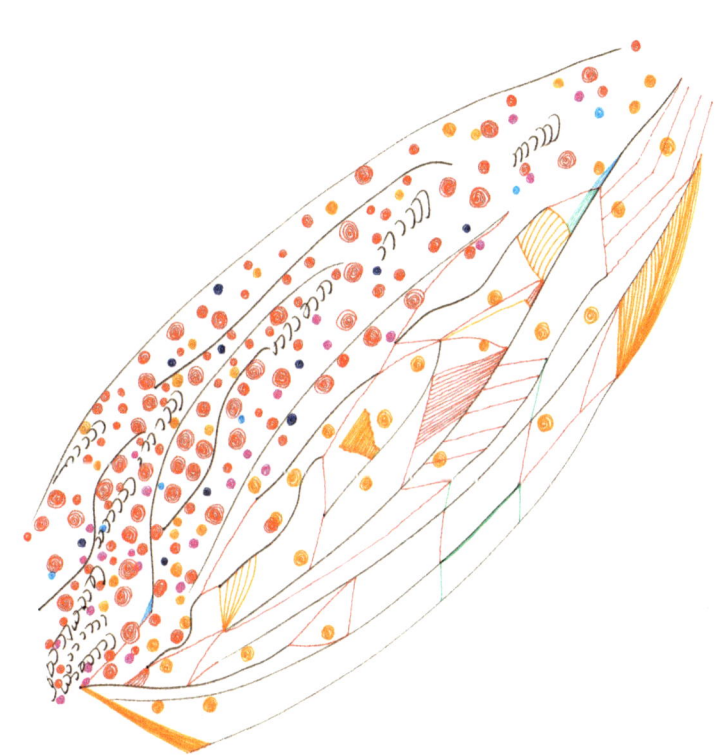

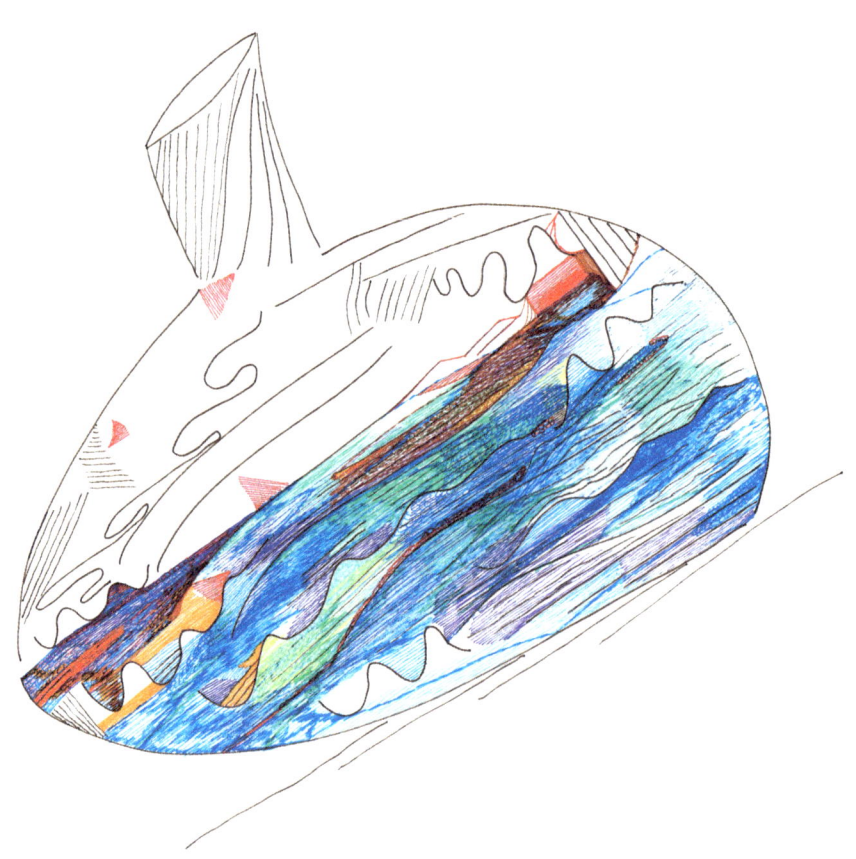

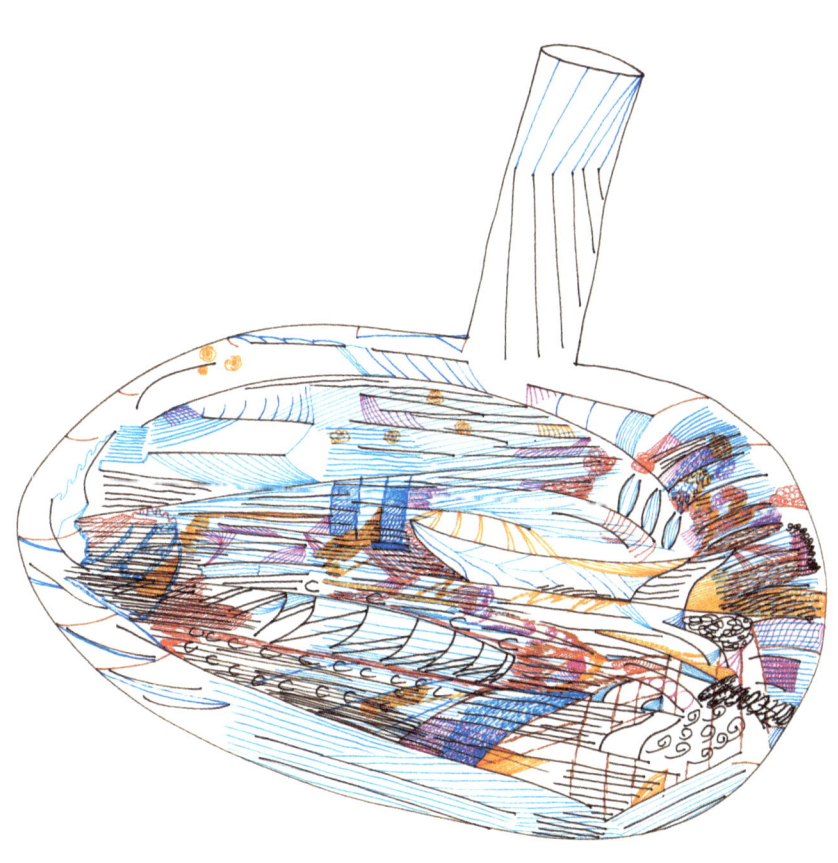

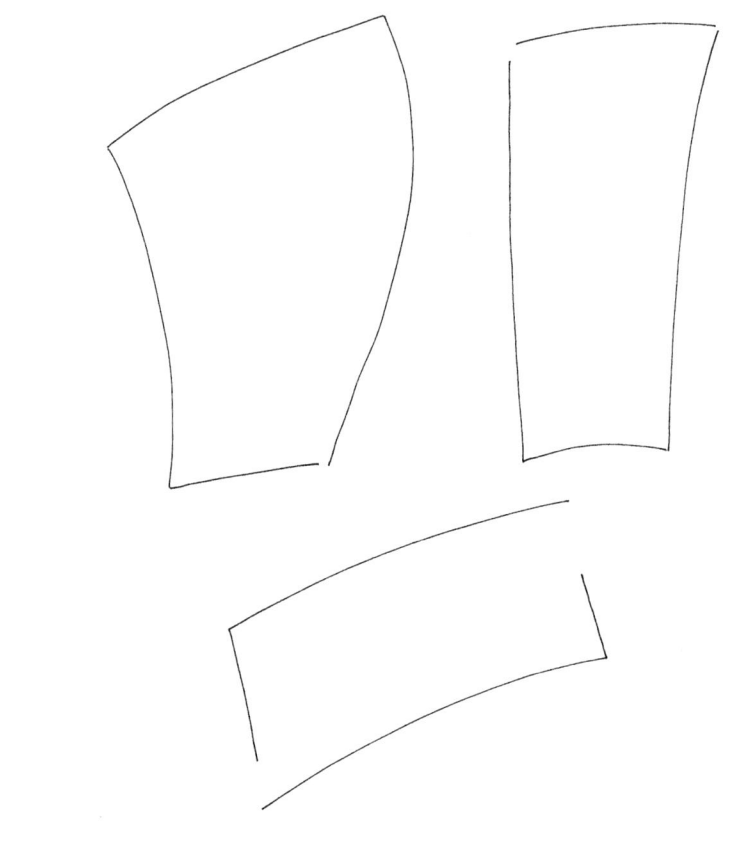

www.ingramcontent.com/pod-product-compliance
Lightning Source LLC
Chambersburg PA
CBHW040748200526
45159CB00023B/1787